HOW TO HANDLE NARCISSISTS:

A SIMPLE TERM GUIDE ON HOW TO HANDLE AND OVERCOME NARCISSISM

Mildred A. Coleman

TABLE OF CONTENTS

CHAPTER 1

NARCISSISM AND NARCISSISTS

Narcissists have a prominent place in the popular imagination, and the marker" Narcissistic" is extensively stationed to relate to people who appear too full of themselves. There is also a growing sense that Narcissism is on the rise around the world, especially among youthful people, although utmost cerebral exploration doesn't support that notion.

Narcissism is duly viewed on a diapason. The particularity is typically distributed in the population, with most people scoring near the middle, and many at either extreme.

The Narcissistic Personality force(NPI), was developed by Robert Raskin and Calvin. Hall in 1979, is the most generally used measure of the particularity. Scores range from 0 to 40, with the average tending to fall in the low to mid-teens. Healthy individualities who score kindly advanced may be perceived as exceedingly fascinating, especially on the first hassle, but ultimately come across as vain. similar individualities may have awkward or stressful particular hassles but have an unnaturally healthy personality.

The Traits of Narcissism

It's easy to describe someone who spends a bit too much time talking about her career or who no way seems to misdoubt himself as Narcissistic, but the particularity is more complicated than that. Narcissistic doesn't inescapably represent a fat of tone- regard or instability; more directly, it encompasses a hunger for appreciation or admiration, a desire to be the center of attention, and anticipation of special treatment reflecting perceived advanced status. Interestingly,exploration finds numerous largely narcissistic people frequently readily admit to mindfulness that they're more tone-centered. A high position of Narcissism not unexpectedly, can be damaging in romantic, domestic, or professional relationships.

Grandiose sense of tone- significance: This is the belief that your donation and presence are essential to the happiness, success, or equilibrium of other people and any enterprises or relationships. " The design would have collapsed if I hadn't been in the platoon." " If it weren't for me, who knows where my partner would have ended up! "obsession with fantasies of unlimited success, power, brilliance, beauty, or ideal love. This describes the belief that you're able of exceptionally high situations of achievement indeed when your chops or capacities give no substantiation of this being possible. However, I'll soon be writing my stipend and running the company, " If I get this job. " " I'll ace the LSAT and get a free lift to Yale law school. stay and see! "

The belief that he or she's special and unique and can only be understood by, or should associate with, other special or high-status people or institutions. This resembles the " I want to talk to the director " mindset in that Narcissists forcefully believe that they should only have to deal with the top- position person in any institution.

They try to fit themselves in high-status sets, meetings, or social groups indeed if they're unwanted. " Yes, the director and I go way back; we 're good musketeers and I know she 'll be eager to hear my perspectives." " I'll be speaking with the CEO to set up a meeting to talk about these new directives and let them know what my studies are on the matter. "

Need for inordinate admiration: The Narcissistic isn't satisfied with a compliment or stroke on the reverse when others offer them as a part of a natural discussion. They demand that others respect their appearance, accomplishments, chops, or actuality. The admiration of others is what feeds the Narcissistic. “ Isn’t it amazing how the color of this shirt sets off my eyes? ” Boasting is of an alternate nature to Narcissists, and respect is generally reported innumerous times to others as evidence of their superiority.

Sense of annuity: Narcissists may believe that success takes hard work – but only for others, not for them. They completely believe that they earn stylish tickets, the top score, the nicest room, or the stylish seat in the house. They don’t indeed have to pass this belief as their attitude

and conduct easily communicate their sense of annuity.

Interpersonally exploitative attitude: Narcissists see other people as tools. Their lack of tone- mindfulness is matched by a lack of mindfulness that others live as individualities with passions, requirements, and solicitations. “ Get out of my way. `` " Do me a favor and give up your place in line for me. " Whatever they ask for, it's in their selfish interest and they suffer no guilt for awaiting others to immolate for them.

Lack of empathy. This is the cold incapability to directly believe how other people feel. This speaks to the Narcissistic lack of emotional mindfulness or depth. It isn't always that Narcissists don't " care " about another's passions, it's just that they're ignorant that others might indeed have those passions.

Covetousness of others or believes that others are invidious of him or her: This describes the Narcissistic constant comparison of themselves to others, wishing for themselves the success others experience, and the false belief that everyone differently is invidious of them. That's how they keep their self-esteem complete. Being perceived as " normal " or " crummy " would represent a pride crack they couldn't handle.

A Narcissist might say, “ Everyone notices me when I enter the room. They know that they’ll in no way be as successful as me. ”

Demonstration of arrogant and proud actions or stations: Arrogance and conceit are traits that are frequently noticed first in Narcissists. This is substantiated by discourteousness toward the positions or rights of others and the Narcissistic amenability to demand and anticipate that others will bend to their will. Like an exploitative attitude , this attitude can be fluently noticed without the Narcissistic having to say a word. They’ll break in lines, use patronizing tones, and act as if they've every right to take away what's rightfully someone additional.

In addition to the presently substantiated nine symptoms, an indispensable model of diagnosing personality disorders, similar to NPD, was proposed in the DSM- V.

This model is characterized by four specific areas of performance in which particular disorders are most likely to be located. Among these four, an existent who has moderate or lesser impairment in these areas would be considered to be evidencing a personality disorder

Identity: For Narcissists, this is an inordinate focus on others to support their tone- description and inordinate reference on others as means to maintain their tone-regard, as well as exorbitantly estimated tone- appraisal and a tendency to be exorbitantly pleased or excessively dissatisfied with oneself. For Narcissists, it's not what's inside that matters, it's what outlanders perceive when they peer at the Narcissistic that shapes their identity.

Tone- direction: Narcissists tend to keep their eyes on the prize that they feel others would prize. They're driven by a desire to prove they're superior to others. This drive is frequently coupled with a sense of annuity that leaves them feeling that they should be above having to work for anything.

Empathy. This area of functioning is what allows humans to connect with and understand the plights of others. Unfortunately, Narcissists only source the responses or conduct of others as they relate to the Narcissistic attitude . Indeed these " readings " of others are out of focus, as Narcissists aren't suitable to directly assess their good on others. They may attend to someone's expressed passions to work the person to the Narcissistic benefit, but no mindfulness goes beyond the practical.

closeness: This is where the Narcissist's true nature and failings frequently hurt others the most. Narcissists are unfit to forge or maintain further than superficial relationships. They don't have the emotional capacity to relate in authentic, intimate ways. Every relationship is seen as a tool to feed the Narcissistic pride.

CHAPTER 2

NARCISSISTIC PERSONALITY DISORDER (NPD)

Narcissistic personality disorder — one of several types of personality disorders is an internal condition in which people have an exaggerated sense of their significance, a deep need for inordinate attention and admiration, worrying about relationships, and a lack of empathy for others. But behind this mask of extreme confidence lies a fragile tone- regard that is vulnerable to the fewest reviews.

Mayo Clinic doesn't plump companies or products. Advertising profit supports our not- for- profit charge
A narcissistic personality disorder causes problems in numerous areas of life, similar as relationships, work, school, or fiscal affairs. People with narcissistic personality disorders may be generally unhappy and

disappointed when they are not given the special favors or admiration they believe they earn. They may find their relationships unfulfilling, and others may not enjoy being around them.

Treatment for narcissistic personality disorders centers around talk remedy(psychotherapy).

Symptoms

Signs and symptoms of narcissistic personality disorder and the inflexibility of symptoms vary. People with the disorder can

Have an exaggerated sense of self-importance

Have a sense of annuity and bear constant, inordinate admiration

Anticipate to be honored as superior indeed without achievements that warrant it

Exaggerate achievements and bents

Be abstracted with fantasies about success, power, brilliance, beauty, or the perfect mate

Believe they're superior and can only associate with inversely special people

new exchanges and belittle or look down on people they perceive as inferior

Anticipate special favors and unquestioning compliance with their prospects

Take advantage of others to get what they want

Have incapability or reluctance to believe the requirements and passions of others

Be Invidious of others and believe others begrudge them arrogantly or proudly, coming across as conceited, boastful, and grandiose contend on having the stylish of everything — for case, the stylish auto or office .

At the same time, people with narcissistic personality disorders have trouble handling anything they perceive as a review, and they can come intolerant or angry when they do not admit the special treatment

Have significant interpersonal problems and fluently feel slighted

Reply with rage or disdain and try to belittle the other person to make themselves appear superior
Have difficulty regulating Feelings and attitude

Experience major problems dealing with stress and conforming to change
Feel depressed and temperamental because they fall suddenly of perfection
Have secret passions of instability, shame, vulnerability, and demotion

When to see a croaker
People with narcissistic personality disorders may not want to suppose that anything could be wrong, so they may be doubtful about seeking treatment. However, it's more likely to be for symptoms of depression, medicine, or alcohol use, If they do seek treatment. But perceived cuts to tone- regard may make it delicate to accept and follow through with treatment.

However, consider reaching out to a trusted croaker or internal health provider, If you believe aspects of your personality that are common to narcissistic personality disorder or you are feeling overwhelmed by sadness. Getting the right treatment can help make your life more satisfying and pleasurable.

Causes

It's not known what causes narcissistic personality disorders. As with personality development and with other internal health disorders, the cause of narcissistic personality disorders is likely complex. **Narcissistic personality disorders may be linked to:**

Environment – mismatches in parent-child relationships with either inordinate adoration or inordinate review that's inadequately attuned to the child's experience

Genetics – inherited characteristics

Neurobiology — the relationship between the brain and attitude and thinking threat factors.

A narcissistic personality disorder affects further males more than ladies, and it frequently begins in the teens or early majority. Keep in mind that, although some children may show traits of Narcissism, this may simply be typical of their age and does not mean they'll go on to develop narcissistic personality disorders.

Although the cause of narcissistic personality disorders is not known, some experimenters suppose that in biologically vulnerable children, parenthood styles that are protective or disregardful may have an impact. Genetics and neurobiology also may play a part in the development of narcissistic personality disorders.

Complications

Complications of narcissistic personality disorder, and other conditions that can do along with it, can include:

Relationship difficulties

Problems at work or school

Depression and anxiety

Physical health problems

medicine or alcohol abuse

Suicidal studies or attitude

Prevention

Because the cause of narcissistic personality disorders is unknown, there is no given way to help the condition. However, it may help to

Get treatment as soon as possible for teenager internal health problems

Share in family remedies to learn healthy ways to communicate or to manage conflicts or emotional torture

Attend parenthood classes and seek guidance from therapists or social workers if demanded.

CHAPTER 3

NARCISSISM AND RELATIONSHIPS

Narcissistic relationships are formed when one or both mates struggle with a narcissistic personality. Narcissistic Personality disorder(NPD) as discussed in the previous chapter is defined by the Mayo Clinic as “an internal disorder in which people have an exaggerated sense of their significance and a deep need for admiration. Those with narcissistic personality disorders believe that they’re superior to others and have little regard for other people’s passions. But behind this mask of ultra-confidence lies a fragile tone- regard, vulnerable to the fewest reviews.

We live in a decreasingly narcissistic world. Hard statistics and wisdom are pointing in this direction. The “ look at me ” intelligence that's frequently promoted by social networks like Facebook has people appreciatively enamored with the image they present to the world. In addition, we may now be seeing the negative goods of the tone- regard movement on a larger scale. So how does this rise in Narcissism impact our particular relationships? For one thing, more Narcissisticity means further narcissistic relationships.

Professor Brad Bushman of the Ohio State University put it bluntly when he said " Narcissists are veritably bad relationship mates. " Studies show that in a narcissistic relationship, your mate is more likely to engage in manipulative or game-playing actions and less likely to be committed long-term. A relationship with a Narcissistic can be hard to manage. To exfoliate light on the common issues, struggles, and goods of a narcissistic relationship, we've canvassed psychologists and authors. Dr. Lisa Firestone.

How Can You Tell if You Are in a Narcissistic Relationship?

When talking about Narcissism I'm frequently reminded of the joke when someone goes on and on about themselves, and also interrupts with, " But enough about me, how do you feel about me? " If your mate is each about themselves, always demanding attention and protestation, he or she may be a narcissist.

However, they may also be Narcissistic, If someone is fluently slighted or over-reactive to criticism. However, that they know more, or that they've to be stylish, If they feel they're always right., are also signs of Narcissistic. Narcissistic individuals may only appear to watch you when you're fulfilling their requirements or serving a purpose for them. A narcissistic relationship can lead to a lot of emotional torture.
It's estimated that around 1 of the population suffers from NPD. However, numerous people who have NPD don't seek treatment and thus are in no way diagnosed. Studies show that men are more likely to be narcissistic. Roughly 75 of the individuals diagnosed with NPD are men. Although nearly everyone has some tone-centered or

narcissistic traits, most people don't meet the criteria for having a personality disorder.

There is, however, a growing portion of the population that's displaying a lesser number of poisonous, narcissistic traits, which are harming their lives and the lives of people close to them, indeed if they don't meet the clinical opinion of NPD. Forming attachments to individuals who parade these negative traits frequently causes analogous torture as a diagnosable narcissistic relationship.

A new study from Ohio State University has set up that one simple question can identify Narcissists as directly as the 40- item test that has been extensively used to diagnose NPD. The question is simple, rating yourself on a scale of 1- 7 " To what extent do you agree with this statement that I'm Narcissistic? (Note: The word ' Narcissistic ' means egotistical, tone- concentrated and vain.) " You can indeed try out this free interactive Narcissism quiz. However, while this study suggests that numerous Narcissists will freely admit to their narcissistic tendencies, it's important to note that utmost Narcissists repel the opinion of NPD. Narcissists, generally, don't like to be told that they're Narcissists. They frequently have a strong negative and unpredictable response.

In Narcissistic relationships why do people come narcissistic? Is it a symptom of something different?

Narcissistic people frequently have narcissistic parents, who offered them a figure-up but no real substance. Their parents wanted them to be great, so they could be the parent of great people, the stylish artist, the smartest pupil, etc. frequently narcissistic people were also neglected, as their parents were so focused on themselves that they couldn't reconcile with their child or meet their child's emotional requirements.

The child was only useful to these parents when they were serving a purpose for them. frequently, the parents of a person with NPD alternated between emotional hunger toward the child and objectiveness.

Narcissists have inflated tone- regard
(both tone-soothing and tone- aggrandizing " voices ") an element of what my father, Dr. Robert Firestone, refers to as the "anti-self. " They're veritably fragile because the wise side of their tone- the aggrandized feeling is veritably low tone- regard, the other element of the anti-self(made up of extremely tone- abhorring and tone-slighting " critical inner voices ").
So, for these people, indeed slight review can be a narcissistic injury, leading to an angry outburst and hopeless attempts to recapture their fragile, exaggerated tone- of regard. frequently, a condescending

comment will help them to reestablish their superior image. Condescending is a common dynamic in narcissistic relationships. This attitude

can be traced back to the needless need Narcissists feel to be above others.

What are the different types of Narcissism?

While all Narcissists are likely to show certain actions, not all Narcissists are the same. There are two different types of Narcissism, Grandiose Narcissism, and Vulnerable Narcissism. These types of Narcissisticity stem from different early teenage experiences and lead to different actions in a relationship.

Grandiose Narcissists display high situations of affectation, aggression, and dominance. They tend to be more confident and less sensitive. They're frequently snooty and have no problem telling everyone how great they are. Generally, grandiose

Narcissists were treated as if they were superior in their early teens and they move through life awaiting this type of treatment to continue. In relationships, grandiose Narcissists are more likely to openly engage in infidelity or leave their mates suddenly if they feel that they aren't getting the special treatment that they suppose they're entitled to.

Vulnerable Narcissists, on the other hand, are much more emotionally sensitive. They've whatDr. Campbell describes it as a " fragile affectation, " in which their Narcissism serves as a façade guarding deeper passions of inadequacy and incapacity. Vulnerable Narcissists swing back and forth between feeling superior and inferior. They frequently feel victimized or anxious when they aren't treated as if they're special. This type of Narcissisticity generally develops in early teenagers as a managing medium to deal with abuse or neglect. In relationships, vulnerable Narcissists frequently worry about how their mates perceive them. They can be veritably jealous, jealous, and paranoid about their mates having flirtations or affairs.

How does a narcissistic mate negatively impact a relationship?

Narcissistic relationships tend to be veritably grueling. Narcissistic mates generally have difficulty loving someone differently, because they don't truly love themselves. They're so focused on themselves that they can not really " see " their mate as a separate person. They tend to only see the mate in terms of how they fill their requirements(or fail to fill their requirements).

Their mates and children are only valued in terms of their capability to meet these requirements. Narcissistic mates frequently warrant the capability to have empathy with their mates ' passions. This lack of empathy leads to a lot of hard passions.

Yet numerous people are drawn to narcissistic relationships. Narcissistic mates can be veritably witching, especially in the morning. They tend to have a " big " personality. They're the life of the party.
They can make you feel that you too must be great for them to choose you. However, in time, they can be too controlling in relationships. They may feel jealous or fluently hurt. When narcissistic injuries do, they frequently lash out and can be cut. Their responses are dramatic and attention-seeking. According to narcissistic personality expert, Dr. W. Keith Campbell, "The goods of Narcissisticity are most substantial concerning interpersonal functioning. In general, particularity Narcissisticity is associated with carrying in such a way that bone is perceived as further likable in original hassles with nonnatives but this likability diminishes with time and increased exposure to the narcissistic existent. " This is why numerous people, who have been in long- term narcissistic

relationships, describe a veritably passionate and instigative honeymoon period in the morning and also a sharp decline as the likability decreases and the tone-centered actions increase. Narcissists are prone to falling madly in love with someone incontinently and are veritably quick to commit. However, this original love and commitment aren't fluently sustained.

When you're in a narcissistic relationship, you may feel veritably lonely. You might feel like you're just an accessory and your requirements and wants are insignificant. Narcissistic mates act as if they're always right, that they know more and that their mate is wrong or unskillful. This frequently leaves the other person in the relationship either angry and trying to defend themselves or relating with this negative tone- image and feeling poorly about themselves.

What are some effects a person can do to deal with a narcissistic mate?

However, you can first believe what you have chosen and reflect on the unconscious motives that might have led you to choose such a mate, If you find yourself in a Narcissistic relationship. Did you have a tone-centered parent? Are you more comfortable with your mate being in control, so you can also be more unresistant? Do you get a sense of worth from being attached to someone who's in the limelight? Does the negative image of yourself they foster with their exams and superior stations reverberate with your critical studies about yourself? numerous people who fall in love with Narcissists have issues with dependency. They will put up with a certain quantum of abuse because they don’t feel confident enough in themselves to set boundaries or be on their own.

CHAPTER 4

HOW TO OVERCOME NARCISSISM

How do I spot a Narcissist?

Narcissism is characterized by a grandiose sense of tone- significance, a lack of empathy for others, a need for inordinate admiration, and the belief that one is unique and meritorious of special treatment. However, you may be dealing with a largely narcissistic existence, If you encounter someone who constantly exhibits these actions.

What's the difference between Narcissism and pathological Narcissism?

Pathological Narcissism, or narcissistic personality disorder, is rare. It affects an estimated 1 percent of the population, a frequency that hasn't changed since clinicians started measuring it. The disorder is suspected when narcissistic traits vitiate a person's diurnal functioning. That dysfunction generally causes disunion in relationships due to the pathological

Narcissistic lack of empathy. It may also manifest as enmity, fueled by affectation and attention-seeking. In seeing themselves as superior, the pathological Narcissistic naturally views everyone differently as inferior and may be intolerant of disagreement or questioning.

Do Narcissists know that they're Narcissists?

However, it might be stylish just to ask them, If you wonder whether someone is Narcissistic. It's generally assumed that people either don't realize that they're Narcissists or deny it to avoid a challenge to their identity. But in exploration using the so-called Single-Item Narcissism Scale, people who answered affirmatively to the single question, " Are you Narcissistic? " were far more likely than others to score largely on Narcissism on the 40- question Narcissistic Personality force.

Are there any benefits to being narcissistic?

Research has discovered some benefits in fairly high but subclinical Narcissism similar to increased internal durability(performing well in high-pressure situations) and advanced achievement in school and on the job. A jacked sense of tone-worth may also make a person more motivated and assertive than others. Another exploration has linked Narcissisticity to a lower prevalence of depression.

How to Handle Narcissism.

Being in a relationship with a Narcissist can be deeply frustrating and distressing. In their hunt for control and admiration, narcissistic people may manipulate and exploit others, damaging their tone- regard and indeed aiming to alter their sense of reality. Arguing with a Narcissistic about their actions frequently proves fruitless. A more successful result is to establish boundaries and emotionally part yourself.

believe that you may not be suitable to control your passions for a person, but you can control how you respond to them. Cutting ties with a narcissistic mate, family member, or master may ultimately be stylish if not the only result. In that process, it's helpful to reflect on the characteristics of the individual to avoid changing oneself in analogous scripts in the future.

What are the strategies to handle a Narcissistic?

Admitting your frustration, appreciating where the attitude

comes from, and refusing to lose your sense of purpose when a Narcissistic takes center stage is crucial strategies, among others. Experimenters who classify Narcissists as either vulnerable or grandiose argue that specific approaches are warranted for each type.

Why do Narcissists make such a good first impression?

Exploration suggests that people may originally be drawn to Narcissists because they feel to retain a stronger tone- regard than they do, a particularity that people frequently appreciate.

therapy offers a brisk, more effective path.

How to know if someone's ready to change

Again, some people with narcissistic tendencies might not have an interest in changing. But others do.

How do you determine whether you or someone close to you is ready to change? There's no single answer.

" Someone would have to believe that primarily seeing others as coffers, rather than people with their interests, is causing them to suffer, and be interested enough in their studies and passions to find out how and why they approach others in that way, " says Jason Wheeler, Ph.D., a New York psychologist.

These following signs suggest someone is open to examining their attitude and exploring ways to produce change.

Admitting the passions of others

numerous people believe " Narcissism" equals " no empathy. " While people with narcissistic tendencies frequently find it delicate to consider the passions and perspectives of other people, exploration from 2014 suggests that empathy, while frequently low, isn't always absent.

People with Narcissism can develop less empathy when motivated to do so, most especially when taking on the perspective of a person they see as analogous to themselves or when considering the experience of their children or others who romanticize or value them.

Someone who shows affection or concern for certain people may be ready to explore further change in remedy.

Interest in their attitude

Someone who wonders why they act the way they do may be open to exploring their attitude in remedy. This interest might come about after reading papers or books on Narcissism, or when someone points out their narcissistic tendencies.

People with narcissistic traits can serve fairly well in diurnal life. Intelligence and a drive to succeed can fuel interest in not only their attitude , but the attitude of others. This can lead to progress toward viewing other people as equals rather than subordinates.

Amenability to tone- reflect

Tone- reflection can be a challenge for people dealing with Narcissism because it damages their defensive shell of perfection.

A crucial characteristic of Narcissism is the incapability to see the blend of positive and negative characteristics that all people retain(known as whole object relations).

Rather, most people with narcissistic traits tend to see people, themselves included, as entirely good(perfect) or entirely bad(empty). however, they might lash out or come trapped in a curl of shame and tone-abomination, If the supposition of their perfection is challenged.
Those who can examine and reflect on negative actions — without responding by attenuating the person offering review or themselves — may be ready for a more expansive disquisition.

Binary opinion

It's not uncommon for people with narcissistic tendencies to witness other internal health enterprises, including depression, anxiety, anorexia nervosa, and substance abuse.

These other issues, rather than narcissistic traits, frequently encourage people to seek remedies. The desire to relieve emotional pain and help unborn torture may be a strong motivator to work toward change.

WHAT TREATMENT LOOKS LIKE

While therapy can help address issues related to Narcissism, it works best when handed by a therapist with technical training for dealing with Narcissism and narcissistic personality disorder(NPD).

Indeed with a good therapist, the process can take several times. It's not uncommon for people to leave therapy once they see some enhancement of specific unwanted symptoms, similar to depression, or when they no longer feel invested in the work involved.

There are several approaches to dealing with Narcissism, but the therapy generally involves this essential way relating being defense mechanisms

exploring the reasons behind these managing styles literacy and rehearsing new patterns of attitude

exploring how actions affect others examining relationships between their internal voice and their treatment of others

The key to lasting progress frequently lies in helping someone see how positive change can profit them helping them explore causes of narcissistic defenses without review or judgment

immolation confirmation

encouraging tone- remission and tone-compassion to manage shame and vulnerability

Changing the right kind of therapy

Many many types of therapy are particularly useful for dealing with Narcissism.

Schema remedy, a newer approach to treatment shown to have benefits for treating Narcissism, works to help people address the trauma of early experiences that may have contributed to narcissistic defenses.

Other good therapies include:

- Gestalt therapy
- mentalization- grounded therapy
- transference-concentrated psychotherapy
- psychoanalysis

Wheeler also emphasizes the significance of group therapy for people with personality-related issues. Group therapy provides an occasion for people to see how others perceive them. It also allows people to note how the corridor of their personality impacts others.

How to support someone during treatment

The causes of personality disorders aren't completely known, but narcissistic tendencies generally crop as a type of tone protection.

In other words, numerous people with Narcissisticity had a narcissistic parent or endured some type of abuse or neglect beforehand in life. The negative dispatches and reviews they absorb come from their internal voice.
To defend against this negative voice, they develop maladaptive managing strategies or narcissistic defenses. Their treatment of others generally reflects how they feel about themselves.

However, there are some ways you can support them, If someone you love has chosen to get help for Narcissism.

Offer stimulant and confirmation
People with Narcissism generally respond well to praise. They may want to do well to demonstrate their capability, especially in the therapy begins. Your recognition of the

trouble they're putting in may motivate them to keep going and increase the liability of a successful remedy.

Understand when they're making progress

Therapy for Narcissism can take a long time, and progress may be sluggish. You might notice some changes beforehand on, similar to attempts to control outbursts or avoid deceitfulness or manipulation. But other actions, like wrathfulness in response to the perceived review, may persist.

Working with your therapist can help you learn to believe advancements and determine for yourself what behavioral change has to be for you to continue the relationship.

Learn what apologizing actions look like

Part of the therapy may involve feting problematic attitudes and literacy to make amends. But the person will presumably continue having a hard time admitting wrongdoing or unfeignedly apologizing.

Rather than agitating the situation or saying, " I 'm sorry, " they may conclude to show a gesture of reason, similar to treating you to a fancy regale or doing something nice for you.

risks to avoid

When maintaining a relationship with someone who has narcissistic traits, a flashback that internal health conditions don't excuse abuse and other bad attitudes . Your well-being should remain your precedence.

Look out for abuse

Narcissistic actions aren't always abusive, but keep an eye out for put- campo, gaslighting, and silent treatment lying come enraged when they won't admit what they see as their due .

lashing out when feeling insecure or lowered

.

It's no way wrong to have compassion, but don't let it keep you from noting abuse or manipulation. You may watch your mate, but you also have to look after yourself.

Don't treat therapy like a phenomenon cure

Therapy can have a lot of benefits, but it may not be enough to help you and your mate to sustain a mutually fulfilling relationship.

Also, keep in mind that small positive changes don't suggest total enhancement. Try to accept and encourage these cases of growth without awaiting further of the same to follow right down.

Pushing someone too hard may lead them to repel further change, so it frequently helps to pick your battles.

You might choose to call out attempts at manipulation, for illustration, but let tone-esteeming reflections go in without comment. Balancing this with a stimulant for their trouble can also have positive results.

Don't let boundaries slip

Perhaps you've preliminarily said, " If you use nasty language, I'll leave for the night. " After many months of your mate offering some kind words with no put- campo, they cheapen you on one occasion during an argument.

You feel inclined to let this go since they've been doing so well. But this can support the attitude, which hurts you both. rather, stick to your boundary while encouraging them to keep up their progress.

www.ingramcontent.com/pod-product-compliance
Lightning Source LLC
LaVergne TN
LVHW052106160826
845678LV00015B/3391

* 9 7 9 8 8 4 6 8 4 2 7 3 1 *